Alan the Hedgehog (as Super Alan) in

Colour Me Alan

Part of the
Earth Art Media
Colouring Books range

In support of

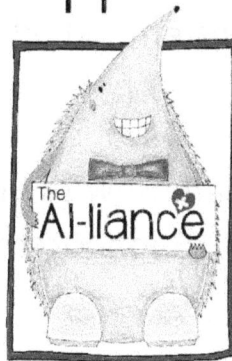

Written and Illustrated by Jon Hitchman

My Fat Fox
MMXVI

My Fat Fox
86 Gladys Dimson House
London E7 9DF
United Kingdom

www.myfatfox.co.uk

Colour Me Alan: How to be a Hog Hero
© 2016 Jon Hitchman

The right of Jon Hitchman to be identified as the author of this work has been asserted by him in accordance with the Copyright, Designs and Patents Act, 1988

Cover design
© 2016 Jon Hitchman

ISBN 978-1-905747-47-4

INTRODUCING...
Alan the Hedgehog!

Alan is an ordinary hedgehog who spends his days sleeping and his nights meandering round the local gardens, fields and parks searching for his next meal. His favourite is a nice juicy worm but he's perfectly happy with a beetle.

He's a cheeky little chap with a zest for life but his life is getting harder and harder! There are so many things that threaten him every day - he's quite often getting in a scrape. If it's not Alan in trouble, it's one of his friends!

Now he's appearing in posters and books, just like this, to hedgucate everyone about the problems he and his friends are facing and how everyone can help things get better.

> These are problems that WE made,
> and WE need to mend,
> For all of our hedgehogs and Alan, our friend!

A BIG WELCOME!!

To Alan's very first colouring book!

Hedgehog numbers in the UK have been falling rapidly for many years. Things are getting worse and worse.

Alan needs your help to save his friends!

This book takes you through a number of the issues they are facing and, more importantly, tells you about some of the things you can do to help.

Many of these images are from Alan's 'Hog Hero' posters. If you need some help with your colouring, just visit www.alanthehedgehog.co.uk and have a look at the awareness posters!

(You can even print the posters if you like!)

What are you waiting for?! Get colouring and learn to help Alan and his friends!

Hello! I'm Alan the Hedgehog!

Colour with me through the next 10 pages and learn how you can become a....

HOG HERO!!

Thanks a bunch XX

HELLO I'm ALAN

HOG HERO #1 - Greenery

Us hedgehogs need greenery for shelter and, more importantly, for food!
Bugs like plants and we like bugs!

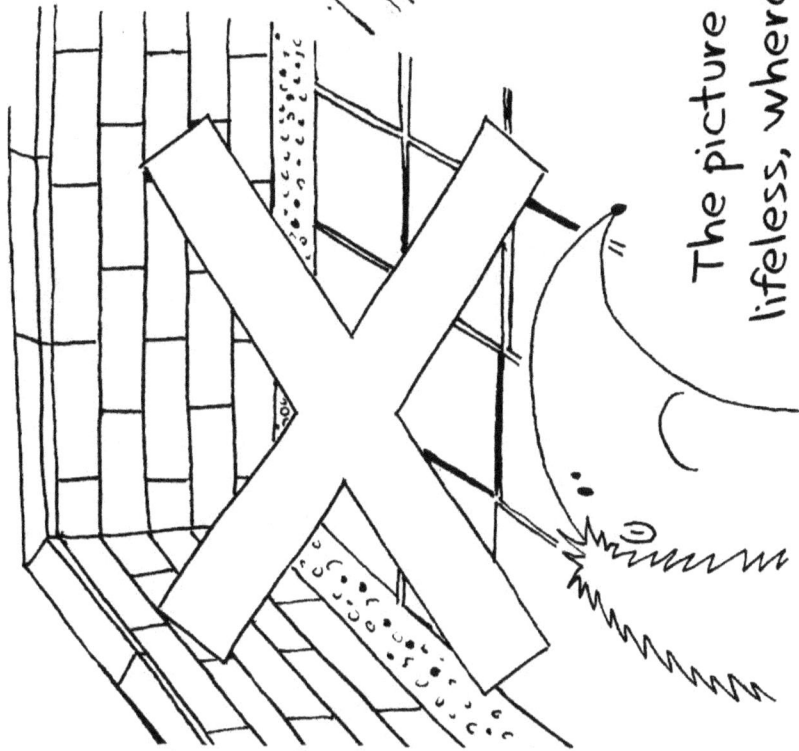

The picture on the left is dull and lifeless, whereas the picture on the right (whilst not ideal) has colour and greenery.

Please be a Hog Hero and ensure your patch has some areas of plants and flowers to bring the bugs by - every little helps!

HOG HERO #2 – Access

Can us hogs access your patch? If we can't, we're not able to search for food or pass through. Please give us a way in – and a way out. Can we get into and through your nextdoor neighbour's patch?

If not, please also let them know!

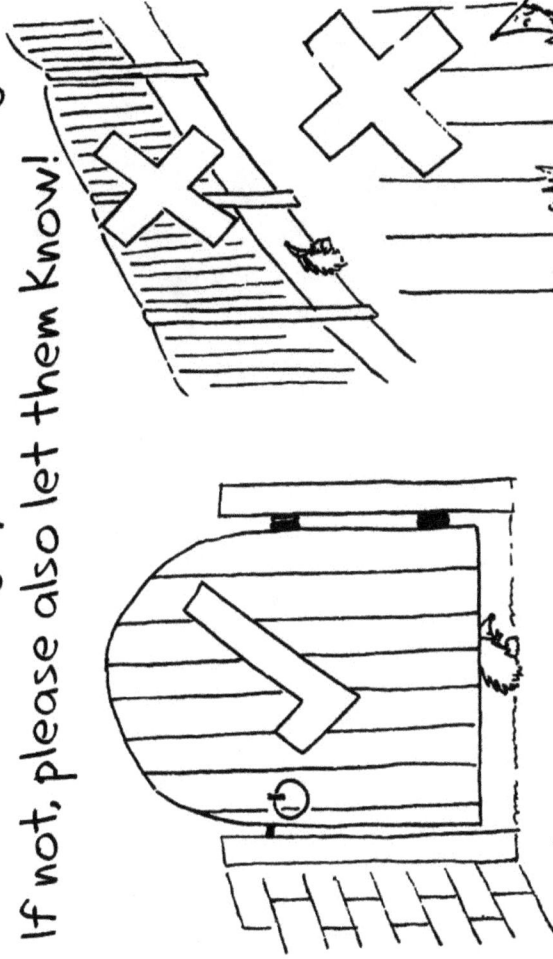

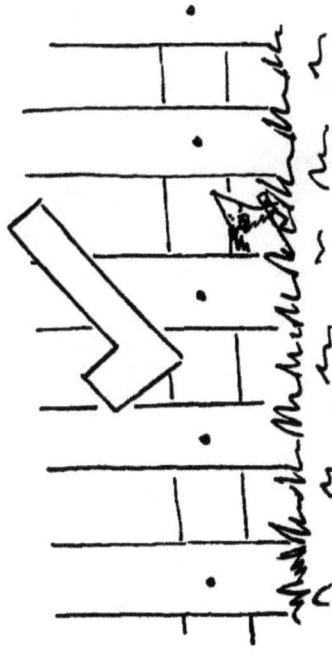

Just one hole is all we need! It can be as small as

13cm
x
13cm

The more access points we have, the more chance we have to come and go from your garden safely. We can come in and have a drink and hunt for food – we help you by keeping the number of bugs down!

(You will also help to stop us having to walk on pavements and cross roads!)

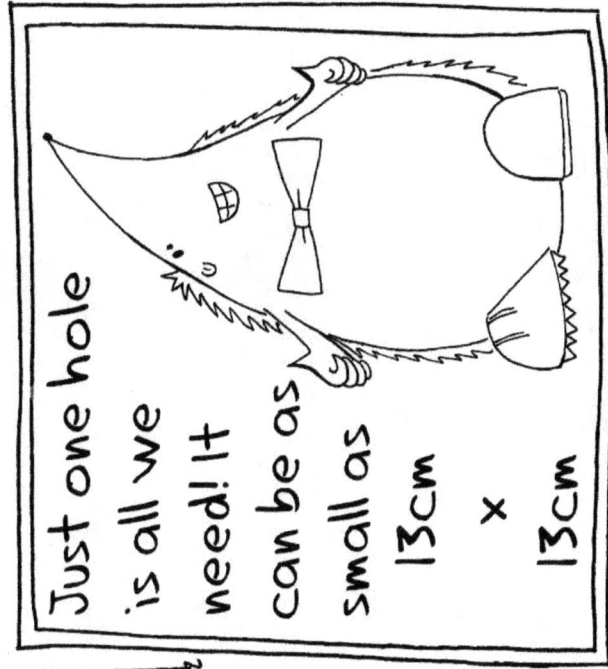

Hog Hero #3 - Food (& Water)

Sometimes food and water can be really hard for us to find by ourselves!

NICE MEATY CAT FOOD!

LOVELY FRESH WATER!

You can help us by leaving some food and water out in your garden for us to come and find.

To find details on what is good to leave for us visit my website - www.alanthehedgehog.co.uk

Hog Hero #4 - Shelter

Us hogs like a nice warm, dry cosy place to call home!

HOME SWEET HOME

Please make sure we have some space in your patch to snuggle up in.

You can make us your very own hog house!

Or we might just bed down in a bush or other thick plant cover....

..or maybe even an old log!

Hog Hero #5 - Ponds

Ponds are an excellent place for us hogs to find a drink, especially when the weather is warm!

They can also be a good place for a snack!!

BUT...

If we fall in, can we get out?! Although we can swim, if we can't climb out, we'll drown!

Please avoid steep sides, and ensure we have steps or a ramp to allow us to get out if we accidentally take a dip!

HELP!!

Hog Hero #6 - Drains

Us hogs aren't daft but we do occasionally find ourselves stuck in an open drain.

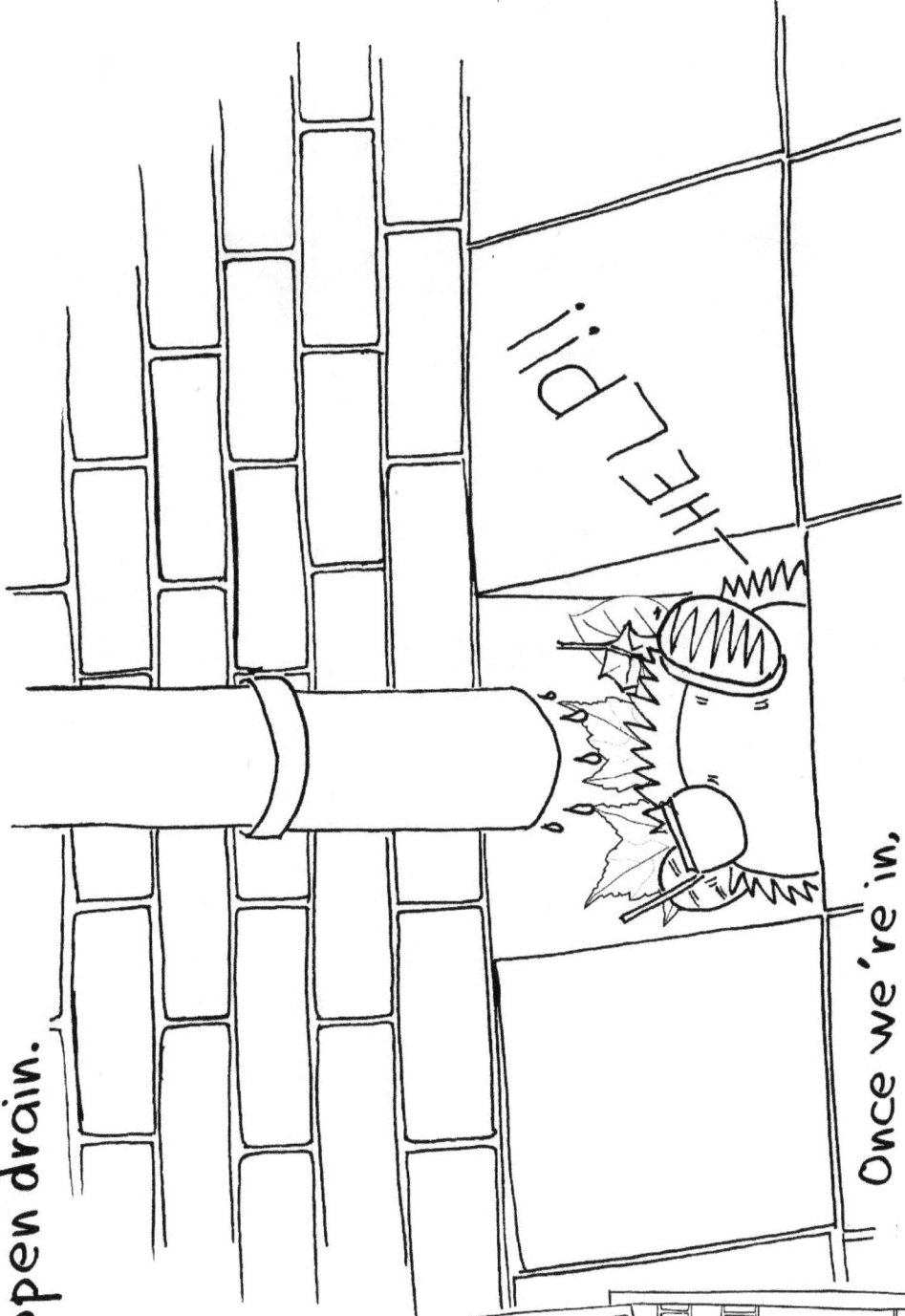

HELP!!

Once we're in, most of the time we can't climb out. If you don't find us, we're in big trouble! Please cover your drains!

Hog Hero #7 - Litter

Your litter can prove too tempting for us hogs to resist!
But that's a bad thing as our spikes mean we can get stuck
in bags, cans, cups - all sorts!

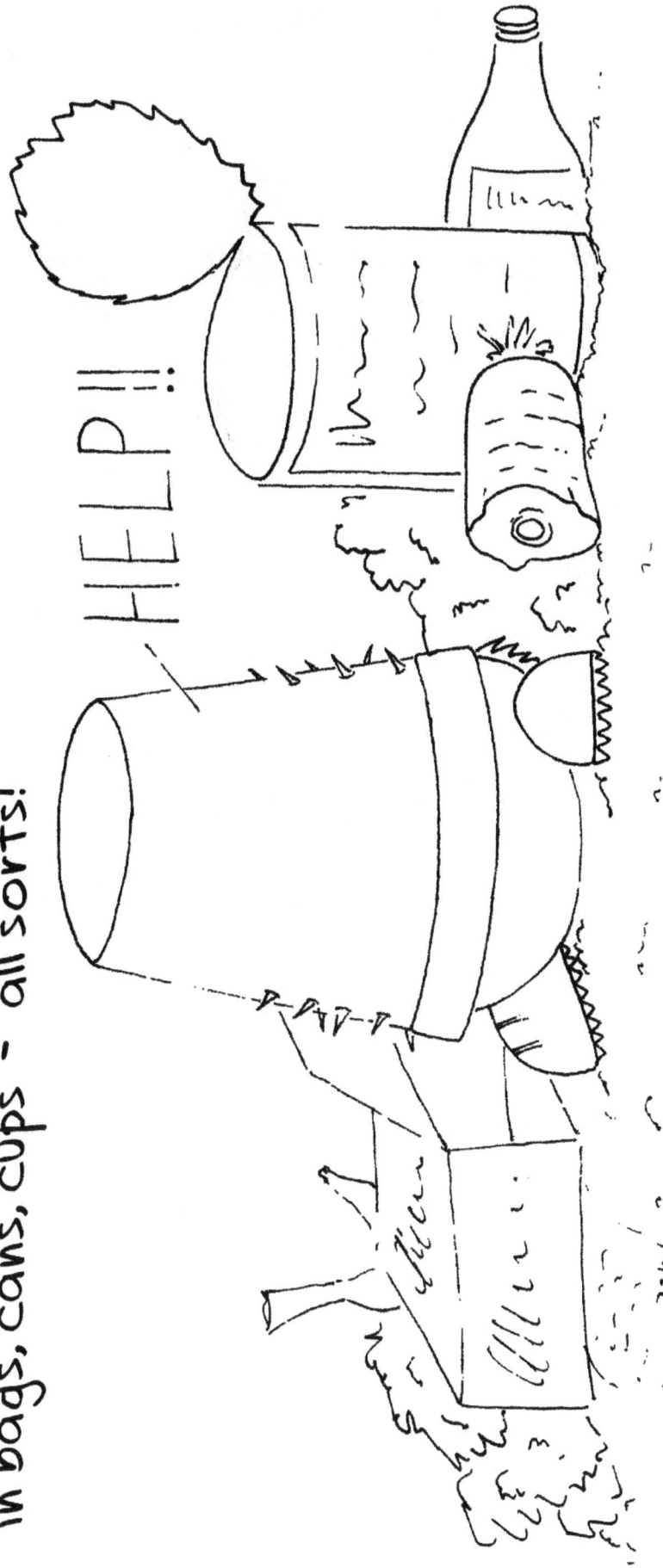

HELP!!

If we're not found, we'll not be able to eat or drink so we could die.
Please ensure your litter is out of reach in your bin, so we can't get
to it and get stuck!

Hog Hero #8 - Gardening

Us hedgehogs are often called the gardener's friend but not everything you do in your gardens is friendly to us!

A few examples...

Netting can trap us!

HELP!!

Chemicals and slug pellets can harm us and our food supplies.

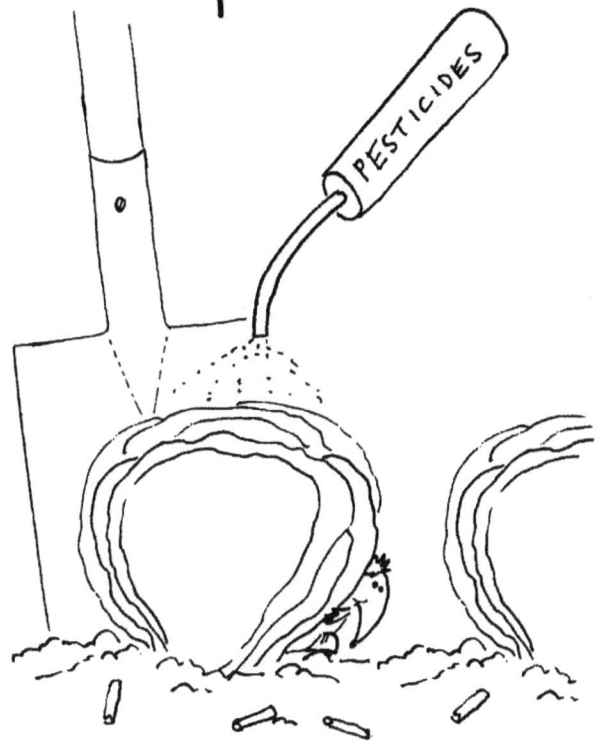

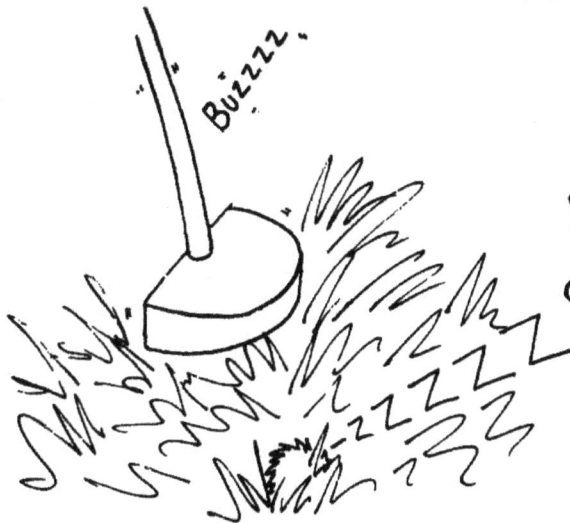

PESTICIDES

Buzzzz

ZZZZZ

Strimmers and lawnmowers can hurt us if we are in the long grass!

Please bear us in mind!

Hog Hero #9 – Pets

Your pet cats and dogs can really hurt us hogs, or even worse....

WATCH OUT!!!

HELP!!!

GRRRR!!

EEEEK!

Scratching claws, and biting jaws!

Please keep your pets away when we are out.

Hog Hero #10 - Rescue Centres

Us hogs often get hurt or are ill.
Often we need your help to take
us to a Rescue Centre!

The centres make us
all better and get us
back out into
your gardens
to hunt for
more tasty treats

You're a real HOG HERO!!!

Please help us hogs

SUPER STAR

For much more info. on how to help us hedgehogs, just visit my website! More Hog Heroes, more help for us hogs!

Thanks a bunch, Alan X X

HERE ARE A FEW OF MY FRIENDS FROM

THE Mixed-up MOB

FOR YOU TO COLOUR

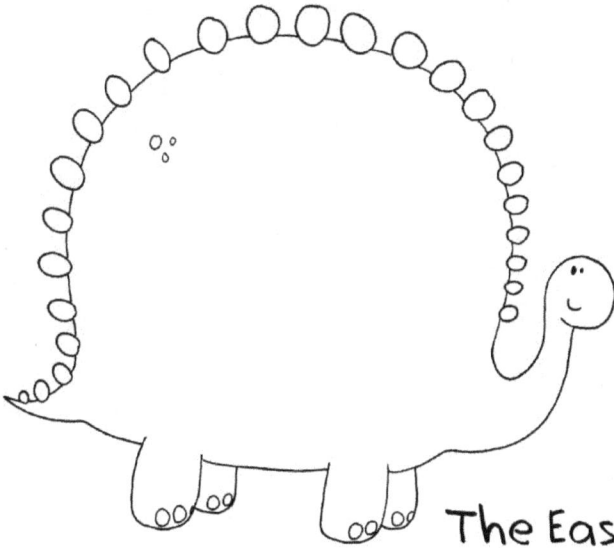

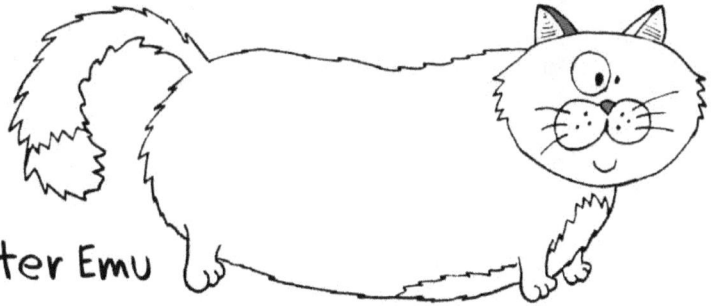

The Easter Emu

Alan the Hedgehog   Rotund Roly   Big Boley

The Shape-a-saurs   Wally the Wartoise

The Squealephant

Country Cow

COMING SOON! IN SOME MEDIA OR OTHER...

Find out more at www.themixed-upmob.co.uk

Alan the Hedgehog
in
The Great Food Search!

Like all hedgehogs, Alan is a hungry little hog. Can you help him find his favourite foods in the grid below?

CATERPILLARS - BERRIES - WORMS - BEETLES - WOODLICE - BUGS

S	M	E	A	L	W	O	R	M	S	A	B
B	R	C	V	D	F	A	D	L	E	P	O
O	D	A	K	E	G	H	R	A	L	B	I
E	T	T	L	I	S	P	I	A	T	G	L
W	O	O	D	L	I	C	E	H	E	S	E
A	H	E	T	T	I	A	D	N	E	C	D
T	I	H	P	S	W	P	F	I	B	L	E
E	W	O	R	M	S	I	R	T	H	K	G
R	F	R	E	T	C	R	U	E	U	H	G
D	O	O	F	T	E	P	I	P	T	M	S
E	S	G	U	B	A	S	T	X	R	A	L
T	S	T	U	N	D	E	P	P	O	H	C

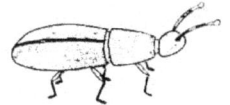

When Alan can't find any food, he might go hungry unless we help him! Find these foods in the grid that you can put out to help him:

DRIED FRUIT - CHOPPED NUTS
BOILED EGGS - MEAL WORMS - PET FOOD (the wet meaty kind)

(If it's not natural food from the first list, please feed in moderation - giving the chance of real food is better!)

And please don't forget to leave Alan and his friends a drink! But please, don't leave milk!
Hunt in the grid for what you should leave _ A _ _ _   (Clue - it comes from the tap!)

NICE MEATY CAT-FOOD!

My Fat Fox

My Fat Fox is a small independent publisher of books and digital media. We are in love with our world and hope to encourage others to fall in love with it too.

More from My Fat Fox

Endangered Lizards Colouring Book
Endangered Frogs Colouring Book
Illustrated by Jay Manchand

Colour to Save the Ocean – Book One
Colour to Save the Ocean – Book Two
Illustrated by Kasia Niemczynska

Color and Save the Ocean – Book One
Saving Animals in Costa Rica – Sibu Sanctuary
Party Animals Coloring Book – Mollywood
Illustrated by Karin Hoppe Holloway

Color Funny Doodles – Book One – Humorous
Color Funny Doodles – Book Two – Beautiful
Illustrated by Hartmut Jager

Where Do the Swallows Go?
Endangered Animals Colouring Book - UK Amphibians and Reptiles
Illustrated by Cassie Herschel-Shorland

A portion of the proceeds from all our Earth Art Media range is donated to conservation organisations. Each book has more details about which organisation it supports and what proportion of the proceeds will be donated.

Visit **www.myfatfox.co.uk** for competitions, news and information on our latest publications.

All our Earth Art Colouring Books will soon also be available as Earth Art Apps.